AX or ASK?

THE AFRICAN AMERICAN GUIDE TO BETTER ENGLISH

BY

GARRARD McCLENDON

McClendon Report
Educational Publishing

Positive People Hampton Academic Press, McClendon Report, LLC
McClendonReport.com
Chicago   New York   Hammond   Gary   Merrillville
Copyright © 2004

All rights reserved. No part of this book may be reproduced or transmitted in any form or by any means, electronic or mechanical, including photocopying, recording, or any information storage and retrieval system, without permission in writing from the PUBLISHER.

Earlier editions © 1993, 1998, 2000 by
Positive People Hampton Academic Press.

Library of Congress Cataloging-in-Publication Data
93-80308

McClendon, Garrard O., 1966 –
   Ax or Ask? : The African American Guide to Better English.

   ISBN 0-9639329-26 (Paperback).
   1. English Language – Rhetoric.
   2. English Language Style.
   3. Black History.
   4. Linguistics.
   5. Test Scores.
   6. Black Speech Patterns.
   7. Black English.
   8. Education.
   9. No Child Left Behind Act

Printed in the United States of America

www.McClendonReport.com

To my wife, Quanica,
for her love, patience, and support

To my parents, Ruby and Wayman,
for the gift of life

The Birth of *Ax or Ask?*

My family, friends, and mentors made
The African American Guide to Better English
a possibility.

- William and Sylvia McClendon for the equity and belief
- Irene Agnel Hayes, Ulysses McClendon, Theodore and Willola Jones
- Duane and Teddy McClendon for the brotherly love
- The Three City Empowerment Zone, the Hammond Development Corporation, the City of Hammond Redevelopment Commission, Mayor's Office, Department of Planning and Development, and the UEA
- Christopher Morrow, a banker with vision
- Jocelyn and Tristin for caring
- Dr. Raymond Drasga and the HOPE Team, Dr. Lawrence Einhorn and Indiana University's Cancer Specialists, and Dr. Sakda Suwan's surgical team for treating my diagnosis of seminoma cancer
- Dr. Dennis Han and Dr. Leonard Covello for ENT treatments
- Dr. Robert Bastian at the Bastian Voice Institute, and
- The Ross Family of Physicians

Inspired by Mr. Vonnegut

On an autumn morning in 1993, I met an interesting man. While eating breakfast at Café Max in Culver, Indiana, I was surprised to see the long, silver and black disheveled hair of the man who wrote *Cat's Cradle*, *Breakfast of Champions*, and *Timequake*. He sat just a few feet away from me which made the close encounter somewhat surreal.

Still shocked and a bit unsure, I asked the gentleman, "Excuse me sir. Are you, by chance, Kurt Vonnegut?"

He nodded with excitement and replied, "Yes, and how did you know that?"

After introductions, he gave me his autograph, a self-portrait, his address, and telephone number. In five minutes, a friendship was born. I sent him a galley proof of my book, and to my surprise, he said that this book was a "courageous effort." He shared with me that his friend, the late Ralph Ellison, received great criticism for writing his masterpiece, *Invisible Man*. As terse as Vonnegut can be, these words were comforting.

On the shores of Lake Maxinkuckee, my life had changed forever. Thank you Mr. Vonnegut, for exercising your freedom of speech, providing a clear voice in American literature. I value our friendship and will always look to you as my literary compass.

Garrard McClendon

AX or ASK?

THE AFRICAN AMERICAN GUIDE TO BETTER ENGLISH

Contents

1. Children Left Behind 1
2. A Time and a Place for Black English 7
3. Forbidden Words, Phrases, Definitions, and Pronunciations 17
4. The Origin of Black English Dialect 51
5. Black Leaders Use Mainstream English 59
6. Good and Evil in the Language of Hip Hop 63
7. Teaching Mainstream English to Black Children 69
8. Expert Commentary on Black English 77
9. Remarks and Statistics 80

1

CHILDREN LEFT BEHIND

At an alarming rate, Black students are left behind in school. The sad reality is that very few people seem to care about children with poor standardized test scores and below average literacy skills. Students suffering from functional illiteracy are considered to be unmotivated deviant delinquents with low expectations. Because these students are poor and Black, they are neglected and labeled as mentally retarded, rambunctious, unreachable, unteachable, and unintelligent. Parents, teachers, and administrators have the responsibility to increase the expectations of Black students, forming a culture of academic excellence.

Parents should seriously inquire about the curriculum and pedagogy their children receive in school. Teachers must question the textbooks that schools require them to use and administrators should seriously observe and evaluate teachers, making sure that their level of performance is a motivating factor for students.

Parents must also begin to take a greater role in their children's education by checking homework, reading to their children, and fostering a productive dialogue with teachers. It is important for parents to know where the teachers were educated? What are their teaching methods? Will they correct my child's English? Subsequently, teachers need to be researchers, treating their occupation as a practice like lawyers and doctors. Professional development and in-service meetings can keep teachers informed of the most current breakthroughs in teaching technique. The teaching profession as a practice also encourages educators to become emotionally connected to their students.

Black children are left behind because of excuses and low expectations. Making excuses for children does not lead to progress. Instead, excuses encourage inadequate progress. Students who are exonerated suffer from social promotion, which can lead to illiterate kindergarten through 12th graders. Teacher burn-out can create a volatile school environment leading to a chaotic lack of discipline. When discipline disappears, learning may cease.

When undisciplined classroom teachers allow Black children to speak, read, and write without correction, the subtle message is that strong diction is unimportant. Teachers who are afraid to correct a child's speech do an enormous disservice to the child, which will lead to ridicule and poor language arts skills in future learning environments.

Schools tend to ignore the ever-present mindset of anti-intellectualism pervading in the Black community. In the book, *The Black-White Test Score Gap* by Christopher Jencks and Meredith Phillips, the authors found that on standardized tests, Black students perform 25% lower than Whites and Asians, and that this gap appears before kindergarten and continues into adulthood. There are no studies that prove that Blacks are genetically inferior, contrary to Herrnstein and Murray's *The Bell Curve: Intelligence and Class Structure in American Life.* But if Black children are taught from birth that everything related to education is negative, we've already failed them before their first day of school.

Leaving a child behind isn't difficult. Public schools, parents, teachers, and administrators do this daily by encouraging an anti-intellectual environment. Schools that ignore etiquette will invite rude and disrespectful behavior. Schools that do not encourage a strong moral fiber will suffer from weak leadership and a fractured value system. Academic environments that do not correct counterproductive behavior will eventually suffer from irreversible apathy and entropy. Subsequently, schools that do not teach standard mainstream English proficiency will produce students who will become victims of social promotion, passed from kindergarten through 12th grade without being able to write a complete sentence.

A child doing poorly in school may have a lack of support from guardians at home. A lack of books in the home, limited cultural event participation (museums, theater, music, art), and a discouraging environment can also lead to apathy. Self-fulfilling prophecy can limit potential and it is a teacher's responsibility to give the child a sense of accomplishment and self-esteem.

Claude Steele's studies at Stanford University found that "stereotype threat" is quantifiable. This phenomenon states: if a student feels he is part of a group that has been negatively stereotyped, the student is likely to perform poorly if he thinks people might evaluate him through that stereotype."

Are standardized tests biased? Yes, but parents, teachers, and administrators must emphasize that we live in a "bias based" society and that most standardized tests, notwithstanding, have biases too. Making children culturally aware of "standardized" and "mainstream" educational landscapes can help to prepare a child for "bias" pitfalls.

In an article appearing in Capitalism Magazine, Walter Williams highlights comments by John McWhorter, author of *Losing the Race: Self Sabotage in the Black Community*. McWhorter states that Blacks embrace "anti-intellectualism, victimology, and separatism." He goes on to say that "so-called Black politicians and so-called civil rights leaders have sold the commodity of victimhood to Black youngsters, teaching them that racism is invincible and that no individual effort can destroy it."

Booker T. Washington once said that, "…there is a class of colored people who make a business of keeping troubles, wrongs, and hardships of the Negro race [in front of the public]. Some people do not want the Negro to lose his grievances, because they do not want to lose their jobs."

McWhorter says that Blacks view educational achievement as "for Whites only," therefore creating a *Black Cult of Anti-Intellectualism*, which deems scholarly achievement as treachery.

Low expectations can damage a child's mental image of achievement. According to research by Abigail and Stephan Thernstrom, Asian American students feel that their parents view a low grade as an "A-." White students feel that a "B" is low in their parents' eyes. Black parents view a low grade as a "D+" according to student perceptions. This concludes that expectations can boost or hinder a learner's self image and self worth.

Akilah Rogers, a former Evanston Township High School student stated that getting good grades is connected to being White. Many Black students perpetuate the discouragement of education by teasing fellow Black students who strive for academic achievement. "Are you going to be White and achieve? Are you going to be Black and fail?" It is time to demonstrate to African American children that being intelligent is a right, and not just a privilege.

2

A TIME AND A PLACE FOR BLACK ENGLISH

Good English, well spoken and well written, will open more doors than a college degree. Bad English will slam doors you didn't even know existed.

William Raspberry

Discrimination has many disguises, but in America these forms are becoming more covert. A person's height, weight, gender, ethnicity, family name, financial status, and zip code can all be targets of discrimination. Faulty vernacular, vocabulary, and articulation can also be used to exclude citizens from opportunities and occupations. Black people must improve their speaking skills to avoid the pitfalls of exploitation, exclusion, and economic illiteracy. Knowing the language of power and finance is gaining clout, not "selling out."

Wearing jeans and sandals to an interview for a bank position would be sabotage. Though this may sound like a ridiculous example, you would be surprised how many people inappropriately dress for important meetings. Similar to this practice stands the case of how language is inadvertently and inappropriately used in formal situations. Unfamiliar slang, Black Vernacular English, and foul language can hinder a candidate's chances of getting a job, or keeping one. Loose language may also decrease the interviewer's interest or respect. A candidate must try her best in adhering to the rules of Standard American English, because being understood is the hallmark of communication.

If eight out of ten candidates are eliminated in the application process, it's a strong possibility that the eight eliminated didn't have the qualifications. There's also a chance they turned in sub-par applications and dossiers. Many people don't proofread their applications and some mistakes can be as simple as misspelling your own name. If you are one of the two chosen to have an interview, you must now succeed in stage two. The purpose of the interview will be to find a candidate who will best represent the company.

Your interviewing skills must be flawless. Your clothes, hairstyle, accessories, cologne, facial expression, knowledge of the company, and diction must all be professional. Subconsciously, the employer is eliminating candidates instantly, due to first impressions. In the book *More Power To You* by Glaser and Smalley, the authors discuss what sociologists call the "halo effect." This means that if you're viewed positively within the critical first four minutes, the person you've met will likely assume everything you do is positive. Within a mere ten seconds, that person will begin to make judgments about your professionalism, social class, character, morals, and intelligence.

Your speaking skills are judged also. Most employers believe that those who speak as if they care about their diction are more likely to care about their jobs. Even though we want to be judged by what's inside, outer appearance and diction form first impressions.

Eye contact is also a very important part of communication. Not only is your voice a tool for conveying messages, your eyes dictate how serious you are when you communicate. Studies have shown that if your eye contact is consistent, you are perceived as more alert, confident, serious, dependable, and responsible.

Why is diction important? Your potential employer is looking at whom she would like to have as a representative in the company. A confident command of the language wins every time. Whether you're applying to a computer company or a fast food restaurant, put your best foot forward. People almost always outnumber available jobs, therefore you should practice your speaking skills with a tape recorder, digital recorder, or with a friend who has a better mastery of the language than you. In metropolitan areas, there are also centers that specialize in the improvement of speech. Employed at such centers are teachers, speech consultants, and phonologists. Many specialists strongly advocate the use of mainstream American English to avoid economic exploitation, exclusion, and unemployment. The consultant's function is to aid the speaker in areas including word pronunciation (phonology), hearing, tongue and lip positioning, diction, and timing.

Employers seek articulate people to fill management and sales positions. Correction can be a pleasant warning and not always a motive of discrimination. Although seemingly unfair, an employer may eliminate applicants due to poor speech patterns, preferring someone who can increase the sales of their product. Most employers perceive that speech is related to intelligence and social background. Generally, one who has a solid wherewithal with the language can be an asset to the company: a win/win situation for both parties.

When in doubt about how to use a word or phrase, save the embarrassing moment by asking a question. Pajamas and shorts are comfortable forms of clothing but that doesn't give one the liberty to wear them everywhere. In formal conversations use Standard American English.

Try not to fall into the trap of actually thinking that you are a "sell-out" just because you may sound "proper" to some people. This is one of the oldest and most successful *divide and conquer schemes* ever implemented. This tactic is so ingrained into Black Americans' minds that we actually believe there is something wrong with sounding articulate. Many Blacks deduce that if Whites do something, then it is evil; which assumes that if Whites are literate, then literacy must be evil. Wayne Aponte, in a January 1989 Essence Magazine article, expresses his disgust with Blacks who ridicule others for "talking white." He states, "Hearing the laughter and being the butt of 'proper' and 'Oreo' jokes hurt me. Being criticized made me feel marginal and verbally impotent in the sense that I had little ammunition to stop the frequent lunchtime attacks." The negative behavior Blacks perform against Blacks is not a by-product but a direct descendent of slavery. Increasing the ability to read will liberate, not enslave. Strong, intelligent Africans were flogged, tortured, and killed if they "got out of their place" and to this day, we still think that a Black person is being defiant or uppity if she possesses good speaking skills. Encourage someone who is trying to excel; do not place restrictions on their articulation. When in environments that call for intimacy amongst those who are cognizant of the dialect, talk as you wish. You should ensure that you don't lose that Black English touch around those who understand the dialect. But in the classroom, conform for the grade. In the business world, conform to be understood.

Don't forget that the objective is to become employed. If you have better your skills than the next person, your chances of obtaining gainful employment increase. Treat this as a rule because we must learn "Mainstream English" to best position ourselves. "Communication is a key to mobility in any company or industry," says Howard H. Bond, president of a consulting firm. The ability to communicate is not an option; it is mandatory.

It has been estimated that over 30% of United States seventeen-year olds are functionally illiterate. This high rate of illiteracy nearly guarantees academic failure in college. Getting an education beyond high school does not guarantee individual success, but literate populations tend to have higher incomes and lower criminal propensities.

Because language skills aren't stressed enough in the primary years, the same person suffers later in life. The rudimentary aspects of learning are critical because they act as a root for future learning. Regardless of the job one will have later in life, we must stress that early literacy helps future blue-collar and white-collar workers. Quite frankly, all employment levels have gone high tech. Jobs requiring technical and manual labor all require strong reading ability, for tasks, assignments, safety rules, and precautions.

Many jobs created in recent years have added various kinds of literacy. Computer, cultural, and corporate literacy are among the few forms that have dominated throughout the last decade, but oddly enough, the most basic and fundamental forms of communication (reading, writing, and speaking) have been ignored in urban and rural schools.

Thousands of Americans are counted out of opportunities because of poor reading skills. Communication is a device used to express thoughts and desires, but so many people do not realize how important each verbal situation can be.

Jencks and Phillips argue that a child in a predominantly Black school is more likely to be in a larger class (with a higher proportion of special needs children) receiving less attention from a less skilled teacher. This can lead to the following. The average composite Scholastic Aptitude Test score for African Americans is 857. This falls about 213 points below Asian Americans, 203 points below European Americans, 105 points below Native Americans, 49 points below Puerto Rican Americans, 46 points under Mexican Americans, and 65 points below other Spanish speaking Americans. Also, the Blacks tested were all born in the United States. African American math scores also suffer due to the misunderstanding of mainstream syntax and vocabulary used in story problems. In comparison to other ethnic groups, low scores among African Americans give admissions directors a perfect excuse to deny admission.

Attrition rates of African Americans on majority White college campuses can be as high as 50%, with many quitting school within the first semester. African American illiteracy can be as high as 75% in some major metropolitan areas because of teachers and administrators who choose to pass students without adequate preparation for the next grade (social promotion). This "assembly line" will only create a collapse in society. Several studies have correlated illiteracy rates with crime and poverty.

Becoming literate is not only a right, and a privilege; it is a responsibility.

The next chapter will discuss some of the common mistakes made by African Americans. Many of these terms and rules of grammar aren't recognized as incorrect, therefore studying the glossary should assist you with your speaking and writing skills.

3

THE GLOSSARY OF FORBIDDEN WORDS, DEFINITIONS, PHRASES, AND PRONUNCIATIONS

Ax or Ask?

Ask means "to call for an answer." Many pronounce this word with the "s" and "k" inverted, pronouncing the word incorrectly as "aks" or "ax." The correct pronunciation places the "s" before the "k" as in the words "task," "bask," "flask," and "mask." Archaic translations may spell this as "axeth." During slavery, many words were changed in spelling and in pronunciation. With Africans unaware of these alterations, language changes among us didn't always follow. Even today, some expressions we use aren't pronounced according to what is considered to be Standard English. Axeth is outdated, therefore we should use today's spelling and pronunciation as listed above.

Ain't
Ain't is a *verb form*, colloquial contraction meaning *isn't* or expressing a negative (am not, is not). This should never be used in formal speech or writing. *Ain't* is often used in conversation and is rarely written, but during a job interview, avoid using the word.

Slang: This *ain't* the way to Chicago.
Standard: This *is not* the way to Chicago.

Ambulance (am-byoo-lens /am-byoo-lance)
Many pronounce this word in the way they have heard it said around the house. Some pronounce it "am'bah'lance," while others say "ammuh'lams." Both ways are incorrect and the person who is unsure should correct the pronunciation before using in an interview. It would be a shame to apply for a job at the hospital and not be able to pronounce the word "ambulance" correctly.

Aggravate/Irritate
Aggravate means "to make worse." You cannot aggravate something that isn't already bad. *Irritate* means "to annoy."

Accidentally
Often misspelled *accidently*, if pronounced too rapidly.

Amen (ay-men) (ah-men)
In no way am I going to attempt changing the way Black people say this word, especially in church during a good sermon. The word should be pronounced (ay-men) or (ah-men) with the second syllable as men, *not* "man." Commonly mispronounced "ay-man," but incorrect nevertheless. Also pronounced "ah-meen" in Hebrew.

Aluminum (al-loo-min-um)
There is only one "n" in aluminum. Be sure not to put more than one "n" around the "m." Some may pronounce the word, "aluminin" or "alunimun." If difficult to pronounce, practice saying it repeatedly.

a.m. (ante meridiem)
Abbreviation for any time *before noon*. Saying something twice can be an honest mistake but try to avoid this "redundant devil." If you say "5 in the morning," this is acceptable. But if you say "5 *a.m.* in the morning," this is redundant because *a.m.* already implies morning.

Alphabet (al-fuh-bet) **Album** (al-bum)
Alcohol (al-co-hall)   **Algebra** (al-juh-bruh)
These can be very annoying words because many say them without pronouncing the "l" in them. Pronounce each letter and syllable, slowly.

Abominable (uh-bah-meh-nuh-bel)
The word means *detestable*. Nearly everyone has problems with words like this. Take your time and sound it out.

Aunt (awnt, ant)
Do not say "awntee," in a formal situation. Feel free to use at home or with friends. The correct pronunciations are provided. In formal speech, think before you say "awntie."

Atlanta/Atlantic/Pacific
The "t" sound must be pronounced (At-lan'tah), not (Allana). The second sounds like a girl's name. Also say (At-lan'tik) as in the ocean. Do not put an "s" on Pacific Ocean making it *Spacific* Ocean. Don't laugh! I've heard this many times. It's (Pacific).

Attempt
Always pronounce the last "t" in the word; do not cut it off by saying "attemp."

Athlete
Do not add a third syllable to this word. It has two syllables and is pronounced "ath-leet," not "ath-a-leet." Also avoid saying "a-fleet."

Authentic
Pronounce the last "t" in authentic also. Do not remove consonant by saying "awthennick." Cutting the letters off of words can covertly suggest that you're lazy and careless in your speech.

Answer
Do not cut off "r" at the end of the word *answer*. Some say "ansuh" and this can be difficult to understand depending on the listener. Also make sure that you do *not* pronounce the "w" in the word.

Among/Between
Generally, when more than two things or more than two people are involved, the word *among* is used. *Between* is used when referring to two objects or things. The following sentences are incorrect. *Tyrone couldn't choose between the three desserts. Julia saw me among one lady.* The following sentences are correct. *Tyrone couldn't choose from the three desserts. Julia saw me among three ladies.*

Anxious (aink-shus)
Please do not mistake *anxious* for *eager*. Eager means "having keen desire or longing" whereas anxious means "full of anxiety, worried." The following examples are correct. "I was *eager* to see my best friend. I was *anxious* to see my bad report card."

Bad
Bad meaning bad, or *bad* meaning good? This word can be tricky in many conversations that require accuracy. *Bad* meaning "good" is slang and should be avoided if around unfamiliar people.

Be
The verb *"be"* has always been creatively used in the Black community. Black people have changed the use of the *"be"* verb, by saying "he be, we be, you be." When you're with your peer group, feel free to use it how you choose. But in formal environments, be careful. "We be going to the store after we get paid," is incorrect. Two correct examples would be, "We are going to the store after we get paid," and "We will go to the store after we get paid."
The *be* verbs are *be, am, is, are, was, were, been,* and *being.*

Band-Aid/bandage
Band-Aid is a brand name for a bandage. Don't confuse the brand name with the product. A bandage is something used to protect an open sore or cut. See Vaseline and Kleenex.

Bathroom/Birthday
Pronounce the "th" in both words. Many people put an "f" sound in there making the words sound like this: baf-room and birf-day. No! Many times this pronunciation is due to association. What is heard in the home and in the peer group can be incorrect.

Band
Articulate the "d" at the end of the word. It's easy to cut it off in a sentence. *Sand* is similar.

Believed
Do not say *believe-did*, as in *I believe-did her*. Similar to *skinded* for *skinned*, *look-tid* for *looked*, or *like-tid* for *liked*.

Between you and I
"Between you and me" is proper.

Brought/Bought
The verbs *bring* and *buy* are often confused. The past tense for *bring* is *brought*. The past tense for *buy* is *bought*. The following examples are incorrect. "I *brought* the bicycle from the salesperson for one hundred dollars. I *bought* this game from home." These are correct. "I *bought* the bicycle from the salesperson for one hundred dollars. I *brought* this game from home."

Breath and Breathe
Here are two words that many children and adults mispronounce. The "th" at the end of the word is pronounced by placing the tongue gently against the back of the upper front teeth before articulation. This ensures the "th" sound. Some people may pronounce this as "bref," but "bref" requires the upper front teeth to be on the bottom lip. This action shouldn't occur while saying this word. Incorrect examples: "Is he still breevin?" and "Take a deep bref."

Break/Brake
Don't confuse these words. They are spelled differently and have different meanings. *Break* means to separate into pieces under blow or strain, shatter or disconnect to make inoperative. *Brake* means a device for stopping motion of a wheel or vehicle.

Buffet
Buffet has a silent "t" at the end. It is pronounced (buf-fay) not (buf-fet). This pertains to meals or food purchased in a line without service. *Buffet* has a French origin and pronunciation (silent "t").

Busted/Bursted/Bust (as a verb)
All are incorrect. The correct form that should be used is the word *burst*. *Burst* should be used in the past, present, future, and past participle forms.

Yesterday the balloon burst.
Today the balloon burst.
Tomorrow the balloon will burst.

Business
Business does not have a "d" in it. Those of you who say "bid-ness" know who you are.

Beach/Beech
If you misspell one of these words, you will confuse your reader. A *beach* is a pebbly or sandy shore, but a *beech* is a forest tree with smooth bark and glossy leaves.

Calendar/Calender
Calendar with an "a" at the end is what we use for dates (month, year). *Calender* with an "e" at the end is a machine for rolling cloth or paper. They are pronounced similarly, so watch your spelling. This is an excusable mistake.

Can I, May I
Can denotes ability. *May* represents permission. Don't confuse the two. Examples of proper use are found below:

Can I jump higher than LaBron James?
May I have some cookies and cake?

Certificate (ser-tif-ih-kit)
I've heard this word pronounced in many ways from *susificate* to *certifisus*. Actually it is a simple four-syllable word but saying it slowly is probably the best measure for correct pronunciation.

Children
This word is mispronounced as *chiwdren, chilren, chillin, sheerin*. The word *children* has an "l" and a "d" in it that need to be pronounced in formal situations.

Colloquialism (everyday speech)
Colloquialism, slang, and jargon should be avoided in some formal situations. This can easily offend people or exclude them from conversation. However, if the situation calls for a more comfortable structure, feel free to interject colloquialism. Once you become more familiar with an individual or group, some parts of everyday speech are allowed.

Confide/Confine
These words have different meanings. To express that you've confided in someone is one thing, but to confine someone is another. *Confide* is to tell a secret or to entrust. *Confine* is to keep or restrict.

Confusable Words in Black English
In conversation, some words can be misunderstood due to context, mispronunciation, or an altered pronunciation. If the word "seminar" has been mispronounced as "seminon," an entire auditorium of people can become confused. The following list consists of words the listener understands and the intended pronunciation of the speaker. Although the pronunciations are similar, one vowel or consonant out of place can change the shape and meaning of a sentence.

Confusable Words continued...

As understood by listener	Intended word
ball	boil
coal	cold
dough	door
guess	guest
jaw	jar
hole	hold
pitcher	picture
rat	right
show	sure
win	wind
send	sin

Consonant Cluster Deletion

Some African Americans pronounce the following words with a consonant deleted. It is important to pronounce the final consonants in these words: fac (fact), lif (lift), tes (test), fine (find), col (cold), lis (list), hans (hands).

Cope

This is an intransitive verb used with the word "with." If used formally, one doesn't "cope," but one "copes with" something or somebody.
Informal: *Gladys coped.*
Formal: *Gladys coped with the terrible situation.*

Copyright

Contrary to belief, there is no such word as copywritten. A copyright is a legal document that proves that a person owns the rights to a work. The past tense for copyright is "copyrighted," not "copywritten."

Crib/House
"I'm going to the crib, yo." If you ever make this mistake in a formal situation, you better laugh it off quickly, or say the word *house* as quickly as you can. Generally this term is a regional one, but concentrate before you speak and say the word *house* instead of *crib*. Slang terms are acceptable around friends, but in changing environments, use the predominant language of the environs. *Crib* also has some negative historic connotations that have been studied by sociologists. Some believe that the Black man uses this word to express his diminutive status in terms of ownership (Blacks being able to own *cribs*, but not big houses). Some also think that this is linked with many Blacks referring to their friends as "babies" (as in, "what's up, baby?") and referring to European American men as "the man." Though I have some reservations about these origins, one could possibly find some value or feasibility in this theory. Nevertheless, use *house* or *home* instead of crib.

Daughter (Dawh-ter)
Careful not to say dor-ter or dor-der.

Dial (dy-el)
With this word, pronunciation is very important because someone may interpret your saying of *dial* as something else. Don't cut the "l" off of this word. Good pronunciation is simply the articulation of every syllable and every letter that should be pronounced. I've heard this pronounced *"die," "di'uh,"* and *"doll."* Be clear in speaking because first impressions are important.

Difficult Spelling and Pronunciation in Esoteric Books
Science, philosophy, and religious texts have many words that are very difficult to say and spell. Use the pronunciation keys for the more difficult words.

Dis
Dis as a colloquial expression means to discount or disrespect. One can make this "word invention" sound formal depending on how the word is delivered, but avoiding this word would be advisable. Some pronounce "this" as "dis" too. You may get "dissed" in a job interview if you use "dis."

Doberman Pinscher
It's not "Domomann" or "Dobo mann" pinscher. The correct way to say it is (Doe-ber-man). Children in the neighborhood destroy this pronunciation. Let's teach them the right way to say it. *Pinscher* is pronounced (pin-schur).

Door
Pronounce "r" at the end. Do not say "doe."

Drawers
Pronounced (draw-ers), this is a word for items that go in dressers and an alternative word for underwear. Colloquially, this is said in the Black community as "draws." Please say briefs or drawers in mixed company or else somebody may not have any idea what you're talking about.

Double Negatives
Two negatives in a sentence should not be used together. Many African Americans love double negatives so be careful in formal speech. Avoid the following. "I ain't got none. We don't have no money." You can easily correct these by saying or writing:

I don't have any. I have none.
We don't have any money. We have no money.

Drowned (drown'd)
Similar to *skinned,* drowned is not pronounced with the extra "did" on the end: drowned (drown'd), not drown-did.
See *looked and skinned.*

Enthusiasm
Be very careful not to say *enthused.* The formal word is *enthusiasm.* In everyday talk, people will say *enthuse* but this is informal. Say the entire words *(enthusiasm or enthusiastic)* in order to avoid confusion.

Informal: I was *enthused* when I heard the verdict.
Formal: I was *enthusiastic* when I heard the verdict.

Experience *(Eks-peer-ee-ens)*
Do not cut off any syllables or letters in this word. Some mispronounce this one (ex-spince).

Expect/Suspect
The words *expect* and *suspect* have different definitions. *Expect* is the assumption of a future event. *Suspect* means to be inclined to think (of, that); mentally accuse of; as a noun it means a person who has been accused, or has the potential of being accused. Next you will find two examples used correctly.
    I *expect* Eugene to be here at 8:00 p.m.
    I *suspect* that Jeffrey has taken my train set.

Et cetera (et-set-er-uh)
Etc. or *et cetera* means "and other things." Please delete it from your written works. It is often over used in speech as well.

February
February has more than one "r" in it so you may want to pronounce them both. The American Heritage Dictionary gives two pronunciations for *February*, but you may wish to pronounce the "r." Phonetically, the word would be pronounced: Feh-brew-air-eee. Feh (eh sound as in leg), Brew (u sound as in you), Air (as in Air Force Ones), Eee (as in squeak).

Fellows
Pronounced like *bellow* or *mellow*. This word isn't exclusive to the Black community but in a formal situation say *fellows*, not *fellas*.

Fensta/Finsta
See Fixin'.

Film
Many Blacks say *fim*, while forgetting the *"l"* that is pronounced in the middle of the word. I have also heard this word pronounced *fil-um*. The words *pattern* and *film* have consonants at the end. Do not place vowel sounds between these consonants. See *pattern*.

Fixin'
Strunk and White's book, *The Elements of Style*, shows how this term can be abused in a few ways. Some Blacks often add to the complexity of this word by saying the phrase, "fixin' to" or "finnah." This means "to get ready..." and falls in line with the colloquial meanings for the word, *to arrange, to prepare,* or *to mend. Fix* stems from the word *figere*, which means "to make firm," or "to place definitely." An example of this usage would be: *I'm fixin' to go to the store*. Be very careful with words and phrases you've grown up with around your house and neighborhood. Using these

words can cause a negative response in a professional or academic environment.

You should say:
I'm preparing (or: getting ready) to go to the store.

Flesh/Flush
Don't confuse these. If you say "he my flush and blood," not only do you have a missing verb, but you also have a vowel incorrectly pronounced. Flesh is spelled with an "e."

Found
There is no "t" sound at the end of this word. Do not say *fount.* A "d" sound is present at the end of *found.*

Freeze/Squeeze
These two words can be very confusing in the past tense and past participle. Use accordingly.

Present	Past	Past Participle
freeze	froze	frozen
squeeze	squeezed	squeezed

There are no such words as "squezzed" or "squozen."

Frontwards
This is a terrible substitute for forward.

Fruit
The letter "r" is tricky. Because of an impediment or environment, some people may never learn how to pronounce the word 'fruit.' Have you ever heard someone say "fewt" or "fwoot"? The 'r' is lost in the mix. Strangely enough, a person mispronouncing fruit may not have problems pronouncing the 'r' in other words, such as *run* or

rest. Consult a speech therapist if you have problems with consonant clusters.

Frustrated (mispronounced "flustrated")
Do not place the letter "l" in the word *frustrated*. Its first syllable is "frus," not "flus." The correction may be frustrating but with practice, a speaker should know not to confuse the word with "flustered."

Go
Present tense: go
Past tense: went
Past Participle: have gone

Gwynne (Gwine)
This is another way of saying the word *going*. *Gwynne* is seen in slave narratives, late 19th and early 20th century novels, and it is heard in speech by those in the south who adhere to Black Vernacular and Southern dialect from earlier years. Delete from formal speech.
Incorrect: I's *gwynne* to the store.
Correct: I am *going* to the store.

Government
This mispronunciation is not exclusive to the Black community. Many tend to say *guv'ment* or *guvva'ment*, deleting the "vern" in the middle of the word.

Grasshopper/Firefly/Beetle
Above you will see the correct words for our friends in the insect world. Sometimes *grasshopper* is inverted and pronounced *hoppergrass*. As a child I used to always use the colloquial form for *firefly* which is *lightning bug*. I also used the expression *pinching bug* and you should simply say *beetle*. These aren't that crucial in everyday speech, but try to adapt when possible.

Gray Areas
Some words are gray, which means they are slang terms, but have been accepted into mainstream English. Such words are *blimp, blizzard, flabbergast, gadget, jazz, ogle, quiz, and snob.* The acceptance and rejection of some words can be preferential. Connotations for words like *dope, fly, magnet, bond,* and *large* are looked upon with scorn because their origins stem from the Black community. What is the difference in saying, "That Lexus is cool" or "That Lexus is bond"? The latter expression is actually less abstract because it pertains to value. *Cool* refers to temperature, which has nothing to do with its value. You will have to cater to your audience to make sure that you are understood. A gray area would allow a term of jargon or slang to be used informally if both the sender and receiver are comfortable with the term. There are certain common phrases that are acceptable because the majority of the speaking society is familiar with the phrase. Keep speech simple for clarity.

Good/Well
Many still have problems with these words, but if you follow the rule, you will not stumble. Here's the rule: "*Good"* is an adjective and often follows a linking verb, as in "The silk scarf feels *good.*" The word "*well"* is an adverb and often follows an action verb. However, when "well" means "in good health," "attractive," or "satisfactory," it is used as an adjective.
Example: I work *well* in the morning. [adverb]
Christina doesn't feel *well.* [adjective --- "in good health"]

Grow
There is no such word as growed as in "growed up."
Present tense: grow
Past tense: grew
Past Participle: have grown

Hanged/Hung
People are hanged; objects are hung. Hence, you should not say: *The penalty for the criminal was for him to be hung.* Since people are *hanged,* you must say: *The penalty for the criminal was for him to be hanged.* If you are referring to a picture on the wall, you should say: *I hung the picture on the wall.*

Homonyms
Homonyms are words that sound alike but have different meanings. Be sure not to confuse words because of their homonymic structure. Two examples are *some/sum* and *sun/son.* Though the previous words sound alike, their definitions differ. Be careful not to misspell.

Hisself
Use *himself* instead.

Humiliate/Humility
Humiliate means to harm the dignity or self-respect of someone. *Humility* means to have a humble attitude.

Hundred (hun'drid)
Hundred is a two syllable word (hun'drid). Many people make the mistake of saying the following:
Give me a *hunnerd* dollars.
Give me a *hunna* dollars.

Hurt
Be careful and note that there is no such word as hurted.
Present tense: hurt
Past tense: hurt
Past Participle: have hurt

Ignorant (ig-nuh-rent) (ig-nor-ent)
Ignorant is a three syllable word. Do not pronounce (ig-nent) or (ig-na-nent) because you will sound ignorant doing this.

Illinois
Do not pronounce the 's' because this state maintains a silent consonant.

Interested
"Interested" has the suffix "inter" in it. The lazy tongue says "intrested." You should slow down and say "in-te-res-ted."

Iron
Pronounced (i-ern). Haven't you heard many people pronounce this word as a one syllable word (arn)? It does have two syllables so say them both, (i-ern).

Irregardless/Regardless
Regardless means without regard or consideration, therefore, *irregardless* is a double negative. *Regardless* is saying without regard; *irregardless* is saying without no regard, hence the double negative. Make it easy on yourself and say *regardless*. The word *irregardless* is not standard and is erroneous.

Jewelry
Jewelry is not pronounced "jury" or "jew-ry." The "l" is pronounced. Try saying it slowly with the following phonetic pronunciations (jew-well-ree), (jewel-ry).

Kindergarten
The mispronunciation of *kindergarten* is painful. I've heard kindergarten teachers pronounce the word incorrectly. How many parents and children have constantly said "kenny-garden" or "kinna-garden"? Speech starts at a young age

and we must realize that we are role models. How can we expect our children to be articulate if we don't reinforce spelling and diction?

Kleenex
Kleenex is a product name for facial tissue. All facial tissues aren't Kleenex, therefore do not use the product name for the product. See Vaseline and Band-Aid.

Laboratory
Be sure to pronounce the "r" sounds. It is more comfortable to drop the middle "r" and say "labatory" but this will hint laziness.

Lackadaisical
Unenthusiastic. This word's first syllable is pronounced *lack*, not *lax* or lacks. Though its meaning bears a resemblance to the word *laxity,* it is not pronounced like them. *Lack-eh-day-zih-kel* isn't a hard word to pronounce, though many have heard it incorrectly pronounced, therefore perpetuating the mispronunciation.

Learn/Teach
Learn is something a student does. *Teach* is what the instructor does.
Informal: *Learn me how to play the guitar.*
Formal: *Teach me how to play the guitar.*

Leave/Let
Leave and *let* are abused on a number of occasions. I've seen these words tortured in speech.
Incorrect: *Leave* the children play in the park.
Correct: *Let* the children play in the park.
Incorrect: *Let* him alone.
Correct: *Leave* him alone.

Library/Libary
Laziness can rid the best speaker of credibility. Li-brary has the letter "r" in it twice. An adult saying "libary" will sound like a very young child.

Liquid Consonants
These are consonants not pronounced due to an overriding emphasis on the final consonant or vowel: hep (help), faught (fault), toe (toll). Pronounce the consonants.

Live/Live
This word has two pronunciations that vary according to word usage. One has a short "i" sound as in (liv) and the other a long "i" as in (lyv).

Loan/Lend/Borrow
Loan is a noun. When using verb tense, one should use *lend*. When using nouns as verbs, you can confuse the listener. The following are not appropriate:

Borrow me a dollar.
Loan me a dollar.

But the following sentence, with the verb replacement would be fine.

Lend me twenty dollars.

Looked (look-t)   Liked (like-t)
Looked is a word similar to *skinned* in its pronunciation. Be careful not to say (look-tid). Yes indeed, you have definitely heard Black children and adults say "looktid" as in, "That girl look-tid good!" Also be careful with "like-tid."

Minneapolis and Indianapolis
Tricky, tricky, tricky! Sound out the letters and syllables in these two big cities and you should be able to eliminate your pronunciation problem. Never say the words too fast. *Connecticut* and *Massachusetts* are two more tough ones.

Modern
Modern has two syllables, not three. Do not say "mo-der-in." See *pattern and southern*.

Names of Writers and Artists
I have an anecdote pertaining to this category. I was in a bookstore one day and a young lady tried to impress me with her words. I walked to the counter with a stack of books to purchase and we started talking about writers. First we discussed a few contemporary authors and then we ventured into history. Out of the blue, she mentions Albert Camus. This was fine but she didn't have a clue on how to say the author's name correctly. Communication served its purpose because I knew who Camus was, but her pronunciation was a disaster. The "s" that ends Albert Camus is a silent one (ka-moo) and she pronounced that "s" over and over. By this time, I was driven right up the wall. Later she mentioned another writer, Dostoevsky, and needless to say, I was "too through." After I politely corrected her, we still continued our discussion. It was a tragedy to see this 34 year old Black woman mispronounce these words, but it proves that we can all learn something everyday, despite age or education.

Nan
Nan is an expression that means "none." Often used in conjunction with "one," this word should not be used at all in formal situations. Informal: *I don't want nan one of them men because they ain't makin' no money.* Formal: *I don't want any of those men because they don't earn enough money.*

Nauseous/Nauseated
The first means "sickening to contemplate;" the second means "sick to the stomach." Do not say "I feel nauseous," unless you are sure you have that effect on others.
(*The Elements of Style*)

Naw
Informal substitute for "no."

The "N" Word
Nobody in the world should use this term. In some parts of England, the word is punishable. It's too bad it's not punishable in the United States. The term is a derogatory term referring to Africans. In Anthony T. Browder's book, *From the Browder Files*, Browder tells us that it derives from *necro*, which means dead. Negro means black and comes from the Spanish definition which isn't deliberately negative. The reality is that the word was created to degrade and to sub humanize Africans in the middle passage and in slavery. The sad end to the story is that we as a people use it on each other to degrade and to compliment. Release this burden from your vocabulary. *Necro*, to *Negro*, to *n*...What an evolution? And you ask, what's in a name? Plenty! Julianne Malveaux stated in Essence Magazine, "*Don't call me a n... Just between us Black folks, the word n.... is often used as a term of endearment. As our society becomes more integrated, others pick up the term because they hear us use it among ourselves. If we want other people to stop using this derisive slur, then we need to make sure we stop using it ourselves.*"

Numbers
Enunciate with crisp consonants. It is easy to get into the habit of saying, *foe* instead of *four, fi* instead of *five,* and *naan* instead of *nine.*

Old/Ode
Old means with age surpassing that of others. *Ode* is a story or a poem written to be sung. You may here some people say, "He so ode, his friends are Brutus and Caesar." Watch both grammar and the way words are pronounced.

Oil
Oil has regional pronunciations. The great mid-western dialect has this pronunciation (oy-el). In some regions, it is pronounced (all) and (erl), but stick to formal pronunciation.

Pattern
Pattern is a two syllable word. Be careful not to pronounce (patterin).

Picture
Pronounced (pick-chur), not pitcher.

Plural Form
Be on the look out for words that do not simply take an "s" to make them plural. Words like *leaf, shelf, and half,* change form when in the plural. *Leaf* becomes *leaves, shelf* becomes *shelves,* and *half* becomes *halves.* Be careful with the plural of men/women. Never say mens, unless it's possessive (men's).

Polish/polish
This word is pronounced two ways. Actually there are two different words here. One means to clean or buff something and to make smooth and glossy by rubbing. Its pronunciation is (pah-lish) with a short vowel sound. The other is Polish as in the country of Poland; of or relating to Polish people or Poland. Its pronounced (poh-lish) with a long "o."

Poor
Pronounced (poor), not po'.

Psychology/Psalm/Psoriasis/Pneumonia
Though they all start with the letter *p*, the first letter in these is silent.

Quarter
Do not pronounce, "quota." It is (kwar-ter).

Quit
There is no such word as "quitted" for the past tense of quit.
Present tense: quit
Past tense: quit
Past Participle: have quit

Racial and Sexual Slurs
In the words of Malcolm X, please avoid racial and sexual slurs "by any means necessary." Slurs do not help anyone. Derogatory words are vehicles used to humiliate people, making them appear to be inferior or subhuman. Avoid at all costs. Telling an ethnic, racial, or gender joke displays a high level of intolerance, ignorance, and inequality. Words are powerful, so choose them wisely.

Read
This word has two different pronunciations. The present tense pronunciation is (reed), but the past tense pronunciation is (red) like the color.

I *read (reed)* many books in my spare time.
I have *read (red)* many books over the last summer.

Regular
Be sure not to say "regulla." Try (reh-gyoo-ler).

Relevant (reh-luh-vent)
Do not switch the "v" and "l" or else you'll have the word *revelent*. *Rel* is the first syllable (not *rev*).

Reptile
The 'p' should be pronounced. Many say 'reh-tile' forgetting that the word has a vocal 'p.'

Respectively and Respectfully
Do not use interchangeably. *Respectively* deals with the order of something; *respectfully* deals with respect. See correct uses below.
I kissed my mother and girlfriend, respectively. (order)
Respectfully, I bowed to the audience. (respect)

Right Fast
An overused expression used in the Black community that is often said when referring to something happening quickly. Actually the word "momentarily" or the expression "in a moment" should be used. In some cases, the word *quickly* could be used to replace *right fast*.
Informal: *Hold on right fast; I have a phone call on the other line. Wait right fast; I'm getting her address.*
Formal: *Hold momentarily; I have a call on the other line. Wait for a moment; I'm getting her address.*

Try to eliminate *right fast* from your vocabulary because if you continue to use it in informal situations, you may use it in formal ones. "Wait a minute" is generally acceptable.

Sandwich
Please pronounce the "d," "w," and the "ch" in this word. It is very easy to say "sam-mich," "san-wich," and "san-mich" instead of *sand-wich*.

Scared
Some people pronounce this word "scurd." Music videos and popular culture also reinforce this pronunciation, but you should stick to the formal: scared.

School/Scoo
Leaving the "l" off of school can lead to a spelling and reading problem later on. For emphasis, the "l" is left off in the Black community. Dr. Geneva Smitherman talks of this in her book *Black Talk*. The dismissal of a consonant is a post-vocalic consonant. We also see this in the word *cool*.

Secretary
This word is another one that can lose its "r" (seckatary) if said incorrectly.

See
Some people say, " I seed it" or "I seent it." You will get corrected or you'll get funny looks for saying these. See the following:

Present tense: see
Past tense: saw
Future tense: will see
Past Participle: have seen

Separate
Spelling this word is difficult because the letter "a" appears in the middle. Not *seperate*, but *separate*. It also has two pronunciations, depending on its use as a verb or adjective.

Shake
Present tense: shake
Past tense: shook
Past Participle: have shaken

Shine
Shine has two definitions: 1) to glow, and 2) to polish. When it is used to describe glowing, the forms are *shine, shone, shone*. When used to describe polishing, the forms are *shine, shined, shined*.

Shrimp
Correct pronunciation: sh-rimp. The following are African American inventions for the seafood: Scrimps, Squimps, Swemps, Swimps, and Swaimp-sis.

Skinned (skinned)
Not *skinded*. There is one "d" in this word. Say *skinned* not *skin-ded*. I still slip on this one from time to time. Be careful. Also see *looked and liked*.

South
The "f" sound should not creep into your pronunciation, i.e: "sowf." Like "breath" or shall I say "bref," some choose to place the "f" sound in south. The "th" is clear and you should use your tongue and your teeth for this sound.

Southern
Southern has two syllables (suh-thern), not three as in "suh-ther-in." The words *modern* and *pattern* also have two syllables. Do not add the extra syllable.

Statistic
This word is a tongue twister for many people. Slow your rate and it becomes easier to pronounce. Break it down to three syllables (sta-ti-stick).

Straight
Be careful not to pronounce this word with the "sk" sound as in "skrate." This colloquial pronunciation is acceptable in music videos and in casual conversation, but "skrate" should be avoided in formal conversations.

Strength
Strehn-th, not strumph.

Subtle
In class, I've heard this pronounced "sub-tl." The "b" in *subtle* is so subtle you can't hear it. It is silent, therefore cut it. Pronounced "suttle." *Subtle* means hard to detect or to describe.

Suburb
Suburb has one "r" in it. I've heard this pronounced "sur-burb" and "sub-ub." Be very careful with this word.

Supposedly
Don't place the letter "b" in this one. It is (sup-po-sed-ly), not (sup-po-sub-ly).

Subject/Verb Agreement
Make sure that your subject always agrees with your verb. If you have a plural subject, your verb must match it or your sentence will sound awkward.

Do not make these common mistakes.

The boys and girls plays the dozens.
The boy play the piano.
These are the correct sentences.
The boys and girls play the dozens each day.
The boy plays the piano.

Sure
Many people delete the 're' ending, and change the "su" to "sho" as in "sho you right' instead of 'sure you're right.'

Sweep
Present tense: sweep
Past tense: swept
Past Participle: have swept

Swim
Present tense: swim
Past tense: swam
Past Participle: have swum

Swing
Present tense: swing
Past tense: swung
Past Participle: have swung

Tear
Present tense: tear
Past tense: tore
Past Participle: have torn

Teach
Present tense: teach
Past tense: taught
Past Participle: have taught

Temperature
Not tem-puh-chur.

Tests
The plural of "test" is "tests." Be careful not to say "tessis."

Throw
There is no such word as "throwed." See below.

Present tense: throw
Past tense: threw
Past Participle: have thrown

Think
Not thunk or thank.

Present tense: think
Past tense: thought
Past Participle: have thought

Try and...
This expression is not restricted to African Americans but abused nevertheless. Avoid the following:
Try and make some money. Try and see if he can go.
See if you can try and buy those new RockaWear jeans.
The action here is to "try to" do something, not "try and" do something. Check yourself on this one and practice alone with repetition. Correct by stating: *Try to make some money.*

Their/There/They're
These three are serious spelling demons. Because they sound similar, you must be careful not to miss these. *Their* signifies possession; *there* denotes location; and *they're* is the contraction for "they are."

Than/Then
Than is a statement of comparison. *Then* means "at that time," "after," or "next." Examples: I am taller *than* you are. Since *then,* two motorists had accidents on the curve.

To/Too/Two
All of these words sound alike but they have different definitions and spellings. Remember the homonyms we saw earlier? The word *(to)* introduces a noun or expresses what is reached; *(too)* means "to a greater extent than desirable or permissible." *Two* is a number (2).

Through
Pronounced: (throo). The "r" is important. How many times have we heard or said, "I'm thoo' arguing wit chu."

Use to could
Avoid this expression and just say, "was once able," or "used to be able." This is a common expression among children.
Incorrect: *I used to could beat you running.*
Correct:　*I used to be able to beat you running.*
　　　　　I was once able to beat you running.

Unique
The word cannot be comparative or superlative. It simply means "without like or equal," which means that degrees of uniqueness are impossible. Incorrect use is seen below:

His Hummer 2 is more unique than yours.

To clean up the above sentence, we should take out the degree, as stated in the definition, and simply state that the Hummer is *unique*.

His customized Hummer is unique; yours is like the others.

This keeps the sentence simple, and does not allow you to get into a verbal war over whose vehicle is *more unique*. It is simply, *unique*.

Wit/Wiff/With
With can be mispronounced in many ways. "Wit" and "wiff" are two ways to mispronounce "with" as "I'll get wit you later," and "Momma, take me to the store wiff you."

Variations in Pronunciation
Making the English language complicated are words with strange and silent vowel clusters. Here are a few examples. *Through, bough, though, rough,* and *bought* all have different pronunciations, although their endings are alike.

Through has the (oo) sound.
Bough has the (ow) sound.
Though has the (oh) sound.
Rough has the (uf) sound.
Bought has the (awt) sound.

Vaseline
Vaseline is a product trademark for a company that makes petroleum jelly. All petroleum jelly products aren't Vaseline. Don't use interchangeably. See Band-Aid and Kleenex.

Verb Removal
Sometimes verbs are removed to place greater priority on a situation. One would say, "John tired" instead of "John is tired." Avoid in a formal situation.

Vulgarity
Avoid vulgarity at all costs. "The thing is, we can often make our point as emphatically by not cursing at all. For instance, you can make someone seem more slimy and dishonest when you call him a prevaricator than when you call him a liar [with an expletive attached]. Challenge yourself not to use foul language. Find a dictionary, a thesaurus, and a better set of adjectives!"

Julianne Malveaux

Y'all
The truncated form for *you all* is *y'all*. The word "you" can be a singular or plural pronoun. Restrict usage to comfortable and informal situations.

Yeah
"Yeah" is a substitute for "yes." Use "yes" in formal situations.

You're/Your
Though pronunciation is very similar, these two are spelled differently and have two different meanings. As mentioned earlier, *your* is possessive and *you're* is the contraction for *you are*.

Your, Yours
Never say yorn. There is no "n" in *your* or *yours*.

Informal: *Is that mines or yorn?*
Formal: *Is that yours or mine?*

4

THE ORIGIN OF BLACK ENGLISH DIALECT

Before judging or categorizing the ways in which people communicate, we must first define terms. What is Black Vernacular English? Does it even exist? Is it a dialect? Could it possibly be an idiolect or regional dialect? Is it temporal or is it a part of permanent public dialect? Should it be condemned or used all the time?

Answering these questions with one broad theoretical statement would be impossible. Studying the origin and code of a dialect is essential in one's understanding and respect for those who speak Black Vernacular English. Teachers have the responsibility of correcting their students' English, but knowing the origins of a dialect can create an empathetic environment. Imagine being forced to stop speaking your native tongue, while forced to hear a strange one. What would you do? Would you try your hardest to maintain your native language or adapt to the linguistic environment?

Black Vernacular English (from now on referred to as BVE) has an origin that probably pre-dates the year 1619. The time period involving the Middle Passage may also be suspect in the creation of African American English Dialect. There is a very interesting bond between these factors and their effects on language. At first glance one might doubt that this phenomenon of speech has any ties to the history and culture of the African American.

Slang in the African American community is widely used. BVE is primarily one result of slavery, since the common languages from the African continent were dissolved by force. As African languages were sifted out of our mental and verbal familiarity, the English language began to work its way into our psyche. Sadly, very few African Americans speak or read any African languages. They may know Spanish, French, or German, but no Wolof, Swahili, or Ibo derivatives. In actuality, a hybrid of language was being developed without Africans and slave masters even realizing it. New words, innovative expressions, fresh ways of phrasing, and unique spellings began inhabiting the English language from an African linguistic point of view. The slave master wasn't realizing that he was allowing

Africans to create a new way of speaking here because of the suppression of culture freedom. Slave masters were confused because they didn't have an effective or suppressive plan of attacking communication amongst "slaves." Many slaveholders tried to ban the singing of songs by slaves. Some tried the *bit method*, which consisted of placing a large block or bit in the mouth to prevent communication exchange. A popular concept was to prohibit slaves from reading and writing but this was an impractical and far-fetched notion on the master's part. To silence anyone (even through force of violence) is nearly impossible.

Once this *language restriction-construction* (LRC) began to take root, Africans embarked upon a new way of hearing and speaking. BVE was born from the cruel institution of slavery, but its devices are still used, embraced, and appreciated by Blacks today because of its effectiveness. Language Restriction-Construction is born from an individual's restriction to do one thing and their ability and free will to create another activity because of the restriction. The construction of BVE was invented from our limited knowledge of the formal English language. We also must attribute this restriction to Europeans that didn't have a formal pattern of speaking and writing English as well. (We must not forget that in America authentic English is not spoken – whatever that might be). Language is constantly evolving. People from England will remind you that west of the Atlantic, English is not spoken; but *American English* is spoken.

Many of the patterns in BVE are still used today and they make perfect sense to one who is familiar with the dialect. The problem arises in the broader world or in our case, the United States of America. Everyone in America does not understand BVE. Some Blacks do not speak and understand BVE. Many Europeans do not speak or comprehend BVE. Because the speaking of "so-called" Standard American English is important in this society, it is in the best interest of Blacks desiring entrepreneurial, financial, and social mobility to be able to utilize the language of power and finance. BVE should not be forgotten, forbidden, nor forsaken, but there is a time and a place for all activities, speech patterns, attitudes, behaviors, clothing, and lifestyles.

There are times when BE is quite useful. Excessive teasing is used to avoid physical confrontation (also known as playing the dozens). Many West Africans that I've spoken with have stated that a similar practice takes place in African communities. Many of the qualities found in BVE are direct descendants of African languages and dialects.

For more detailed information, seek studies by Dr. Geneva Smitherman, a speech and African Studies expert. She has studied languages from Africa and gives several examples in her research.

African speech characteristics that have been fused into the English language are profound and very useful. When speaking Standard American English (SAE), one can lose something in the translation from BVE to SAE. Here's an example. Two ladies are talking about a man who has been unkind to one of the ladies. First the conversation in Black Vernacular English.

Speaker 1: What's up girl? Whatchu gon' do wit 'em?
Speaker 2: Girl, he been iggy from the gizzy.
Speaker 1: 'Scuse me, girl, whatchu gone do?
Speaker 2: Amma drop the nizzle, next week!
Speaker 1: Dats whatchu sed las week.

Now here's the conversation in Standard American English.

Speaker 1: What's going on friend? What are you going to do with him?
Speaker 2: Girlfriend, he hasn't been acting right since the beginning.
Speaker 1: Excuse me, friend, so what are you going to do?
Speaker 2: I'm going to break up with that loser next week!
Speaker 1: That's what you told me last week.

The differences between the words, the usage, the accents, and the rhythm are clearly identified here. The message is conveyed in BVE and as you can see, there is a great deal of emphasis lost in the translation to Standard English. In the neighborhood, I prefer using BVE because it is comfortable, communicable, colorful, and vast. The skill is in the ability to shift gears into the "other English" when needed.

Shifting gears can be called several things. Some would say that it is *selling out* (assimilation). Others might call verbal gear shifting a form of adaptation or "code switching." It is clear that this skill (the ability to change from BVE to SAE back to BVE) is what W.E.B. DuBois once alluded to as the *Veil.* The *Veil* is the dual consciousness that inhabits the African-American. He explains this in his book, *The Souls of Black Folk:*

> ...the Negro is a sort of seventh son, born with a veil, and gifted with second-sight in this American world, -- a world which yields him no true self-consciousness, but only lets him see himself through the revelation of the other world. It is a peculiar sensation, this double-consciousness, this sense of always looking at one's self through the eyes of others, of measuring one's soul by the tape of a world that looks on in amused contempt and pity. One ever feels his twoness, -- an American, a Negro; two souls, two thoughts, two unreconciled strivings; two warring ideals in one dark body, whose dogged strength alone keeps it from being torn asunder.

This DuBois quote sums up the African American experience and its many complexities. The question of dialect switching can be equally complex, but great concern should be taken in knowing both dialects, and having the knowledge to use them at the *right* times.

Frederick Douglass also teaches us a lesson in his autobiographical essays and letters. Africans were forbidden to learn how to read and he emphatically points out the Black child's need for literacy in this poignant quote from his slave master.

> If you teach that n.... how to read, there would be no keeping him. Learning would *spoil* the best n..... in the world. It would forever unfit him to be a slave. If you give a n.... an inch, he will take an ell (45 inches). A n..... should know nothing but to obey his master--to do as he is told to do.

Frederick Douglass goes on to say,

> I now understood what had been to me a most perplexing difficulty--to wit, the slave masters power to enslave the black man (is to keep him illiterate).

What makes us so arrogant as to think that learning the language of power and finance isn't important today? Forced illiteracy was also a contribution to perpetuating slavery. The ability to read is the most powerful force in one's academic life.

5

BLACK LEADERS USE MAINSTREAM ENGLISH

Our most prominent Black leaders speak Standard American English. Even those who claim to promote the constant use of Black English, make it a point to speak as mainstream as possible to embrace mass audiences.

Dr. Martin Luther King, Jr., had epitomizing enunciation and verbal expression. King's words sounded like music and his metaphors and similes were far better than many of the greatest poets.

The diction of Malcolm X was nearly flawless and he achieved such eloquence by his own volition (reading the dictionary and various books by philosophers, scientists, and religious figures while in prison). Malcolm realized that the best way to impart knowledge was to use mainstream English. Although never attending a formal university system, he was often contracted to speak at Ivy League institutions. His verbal precision was magnificent.

In the academic and creative arenas, Maya Angelou's poetry delivery, Heru Petah's novelic genius, Tina Ansa McElroy's articulation, and the rhetorical skills of Cornel West, Michael Eric Dyson and Na'im Akbar, have significantly impressed and influenced many of us. These individuals capture the essence of our culture and history in their works. In public environments, they also speak Standard English.

Dr. W.E.B. DuBois, James Baldwin, Richard Wright, Dr. Carter G. Woodson, and Ralph Ellison have shown us the social and psychological problems that have plagued the African American with their exemplary writing. To this day, works from these men still resonant within the African American community.

Even superstar musicians, entertainers, and athletes find it in their best interest to command consistent mainstream English. Good diction attracts more endorsements, interviews, appearances, and exposure. Black athletes who use understandable diction can increase their potential for speaking opportunities which can lead to careers beyond their athletic ones. Wouldn't it be embarrassing if Black athletes could not speak Standard

American English? Haven't we all felt that nervous tension when a Black athlete steps to the microphone to make a comment? Unfortunately, we assume that the speaker will sound illiterate and terrifyingly inarticulate? Today's players have satisfactory speaking abilities, but there are still a few of us that have great difficulty with the English language. Better speaking skills for athletes can lead to more *playing time* on the microphone during interviews. This, in turn, can lead to commercial endorsements.

There is a direct connection between articulation and potential income. It is no accident why Muhammad Ali and Sugar Ray Leonard were able to command more money than other boxers of their time. Sure, their boxing abilities may have been more consistent with longer winning streaks, but spectators were also drawn by their eloquence. Don King can promote fights better than anyone else in the world because he has great mastery of the language and its power to manipulate the public into becoming fanatical about seeing a fight. His words are so convincing, he makes the boxing fan feel guilty if he or she misses the fight via satellite.

We must start realizing in the words of Jesse Jackson that *excellence transcends race*. Speaking Standard American English isn't *selling out*, or being a *Tom*. Using your best diction will enable you to get ahead in the United States. Oprah Winfrey, Ahmad Rashad, Bill Cosby, Cornel West, Michael Eric Dyson, Henry Louis Gates, Greg and Bryant Gumble, John Rogers and Jawanza Kunjufu wouldn't have achieved great commercial and academic success if they exercised poor communication skills. We as a people have to take the high road that will lead us to the promised land, the land of milk and honey, and the road that leads to our success as a people.

Most children would like to be successful someday. What we as adults have to do is to identify what success is and to show our children the measures that have to be taken to achieve a level of success. Use of language is one of those measures. There is nothing wrong with a child wanting to be a professional basketball player, but the odds are too great to take that chance alone (just a fraction of the three million NCAA athletes make it into the pros – lots of applicants, very few jobs).

Let's teach our children and educate our adults about the pitfalls we all suffer in this war against illiteracy. Study the examples in this book and also J.L. Dillard's *Black English* and Dr. Geneva Smitherman's *Black Talk [Words and Phrases from the Hood to the Amen Corner]*.

6

GOOD AND EVIL IN THE LANGUAGE OF HIP HOP

Rap music is Black America's T.V. station.
Chuck D.

In the world of rap music there are many positive and negative signs. This chapter will focus on the perils and triumphs of rap's language. I will have to criticize some rap artists intensely because of their destructive nature. Later in the chapter, I will sing praises and give rap its kudos.

Besides many rap artists referring to women as "female dogs" and "easy visits" there are many other evils in this industry's warped view of its own people. Language is also altered and we must be mindful of intentional misspellings on CD covers, twisted definitions, and mispronunciation in songs. All of these characteristics attribute to a new dialect that is amusing and entertaining. But if children are unable to distinguish between the dialect of rap (saturated with Black Vernacular English) and the *great Midwestern dialect,* you will have a child that will confuse these same concepts in school, church, home, and among friends. It should be obvious why this can be detrimental.

Whether it's choosing to say *for sure, fuh sheezy or fo shizzle my nizzle*, we must teach children that there is a time and a place for dialects. A popular spelling for the word "fat" on many rap CD covers is "phat" as in the company created by Russell Simmons: PHAT FARM. It is spelled this way for three reasons: 1) to rebel against traditional English, 2) because it's different (fashionable) and, 3) it is phonetically pronounced the same as "fat." Small children and adolescents are heavily influenced by rap music and it is important for you to teach your child the difference between standard and non-standard English for spelling, vocabulary tests, and daily pronunciation.

The book, *The Elements of Style,* drives this point home even more by listing other more universal examples. Strunk and White state:

> In ordinary composition, use orthodox spelling. Do not write *nite* for *night, thru* for *through, pleez* for *please,* unless you plan to

introduce a complete system of simplified spelling and are prepared to take the consequences.

Stick to the rules of English to avoid looking inarticulate and unintelligent. Be on the lookout for other terms used in rap that may not be considered standard. *Ice, bling, fuh shizzle, bustin', jackin', er-body (instead of everybody), af-fleet, wack, nine m, ax instead of ask, gat , boo, blowin' up, trues, dubs, knobs, shorty, squeeze, knuckles, "G," rock, Joe, slippin', mack, drop, low rider, philly, slim, dog, trippin', scope,* and the many other expressions and words that are used in rap, can be colorful and comfortable in your environment. One should restrict the usage in the situations we've mentioned earlier.

Most rap music is very degrading to Black people. Women take major punishment, morals get thrown out of the window, and the respect for the African American also becomes diminutive. Most rap videos depict young Black men as unemployed or drug dealing, abusers of women with a serious appetite for alcohol and SUVs with enormous rims. Sadly, many non-Blacks think that the majority of Black people live like this. Not true. Where are the rappers with decent clothes, a belt to hold up their pants, grammar, and videos that don't exist in "da hood"? Do all Black people live in war torn ghettoes, replete with drugs, low-riders, and half-dressed women? Do these rappers have mothers and sisters that they respect enough to pay tribute? What's more, do these rappers ever articulate in a manner that can be understood by most people? They aren't obligated to, but children need to know that these video images are limited and inaccurate depictions of "life in the hood," because most of these *rappers* live in the suburbs. Being able to distinguish the good from the bad is the key. There is a time and place for rap lingo, but it's not in a formal letter to a corporation or on a standardized test in school. Make sure your child is reading and that the child understands the difference between rap's English and Standard American English. If you allow your child to listen to rap, you may want to listen as well.

On the other hand, some rappers provide positive messages in their lyrics. Some rappers choose to express messages such as warning young people of the medical, moral, and emotional dangers of pre-marital sex, staying in school, knowledge of self, and the promotion of reading. Kanye West, Outkast, The Roots, Lauren Hill, Missy Elliot, Common, Mos Def, Latifah, and others are all champions of positive messages. Just as Elie Wiesel would feel obligated to discuss the Holocaust, rap artists feel the obligation to discuss items that concern the Black community and slavery's *middle passage*. Jazz musician, Donald Byrd, defended Rap music by making this statement, "Rap music is a poetic form criticized because many who condemn it cannot do it successfully."

Rappers like Tupac and Biggie (before their untimely deaths), 50 Cent, Fabulous, Ice Cube, Snoop Dog, Ice T, Dr. Dre', Eminem, Mystikal, the East Side Boys, Master P, and DMX have more pugnacious and obscene content, but their lyrics state the truth about the treatment of Black Americans and how some Black people feel. Others are considered gentle in lyrical content but manage to instill responsible behavior in their CDs from treating women with respect to becoming a productive citizen in society. Rap music is a medium that influences heavily on our children and we must monitor (not censor) the lyrics they digest.

For your child's sake, show the distinction between what's right and wrong lyrically. Some rappers exaggerate to reinforce a point. Children should be taught to realize that rap artists are entertainers. This is the responsibility of the parents, even though they may not listen to all of the rap music in the child's collection.

Rap's strongest ally is the music (beat, bass line, and samples). Sometimes lyrics aren't understandable because of music drowning out the rapper or the confusion of regional dialect. But most lyrics are easily heard and can be offensive. It is unfortunate, that most rappers are African American buffoons who choose to curse out their audience for a paycheck. Soon the day will come when more of our music is edifying, as it once was in the not so distant past. Motown, Stax, and T-Neck must visit our world again.

7

TEACHING MAINSTREAM ENGLISH TO BLACK CHILDREN

There are thousands of teachers in the United States who do not teach Standard English to their students. I have visited over 25 school systems and the atrocious English spoken by some of America's certified teachers, borders on the ridiculous. Today, it is imperative that English teachers make a concerted effort to not only speak Standard English in the classroom, but to also spend extra time teaching their students the difference between what is accepted in the academic world, and what is accepted in their neighborhoods. It is also crucial for teachers to speak Standard English.

Some school systems are proficient and prolific producers of high school graduates who cannot read a job application, a contract, or a book written for someone six grades lower than the "graduate." Sadly, some Black school districts continue to socially promote, and many students will never experience a highly qualified teacher.

Literacy is the first element needed in the equation of obtaining a good education. In this age of cyberspace, not only will a person have to be literate in terms of reading a book, but technical demands will place a strain on those who aren't able to decipher more sophisticated manuals, more esoteric instructions, and incessant advances in computer software. The days of numerous factory jobs are just about over and by the year 2010, it has been estimated that over 50% of American citizens will have to create their own job, consisting of office tools used at home, to generate family income. Are students ready for this transformation?

It sounds a bit intimidating, but literacy is no longer a monolithic concept. Computer literacy is just as important as being able to read a sentence. Additionally, having a personal computer is going to be mandatory for survival. This is crucial because statistically, African Americans have the lowest number of updated computers per household than any other ethnic group. Teachers in affluent districts are fortunate with the new educator programs that provide computers at discount rates for participating schools.

Unfortunately, there are many teachers and students lacking computer training. Philanthropic funding and Title I funds for disadvantaged students can help to bridge the divide, but students will still need teachers who are computer literate and who take pride in giving students an intellectual setting. This also means correcting students when they deliver incorrect answers. With the mastery of the English language (the language of power and finance) along with computer literacy, a child can take full advantage of the limitless assets a school system has to offer.

English skills are fundamental. Even though there are Black children diagnosed as LEP (limited-English proficient), EMR (educable mentally retarded), and NEP (non-English proficient) steering them in the direction of mainstream English is imperative. Hopefully there aren't any Empiricists and Romantic ideologists teaching in our schools today. Empiricists believed that Africans were brute, savage animals who didn't have the cortical capacity for human language. Empiricists such as John Locke and Carolus Linnaeus believed that Africans had a language similar to primates (chimps and gorillas). Romanticists believed that Africans were simple, unsophisticated children incapable of understanding "esoteric" speech patterns. This is utterly ridiculous. Africans aren't inherently nor genetically inferior, but there are some who would like to perpetuate such falsehoods.

Choosing not to use mainstream American English is a hindrance for thousands, which was cited in a USA Today article entitled "The Dumbing of the American Mind." This article stated that the average 17-year old could not successfully balance a checkbook, do relatively simple multiplication and division problems, or spend a concentrated block of time in order to read a book.

In Eleanor Wilson Orr's insightful book, *Twice as Less: Does Black English Stand Between Black Students and Success in Math and Science*, she noted that the multitude of students misunderstood prepositions, conjunctions, and relative pronouns which obviously alter the meaning of story problems. But if teachers were sensitive to the nuances and rhythms of Black English as well as the structure of the language, there would be more empathy for the student. One problem is the teacher's lack of responsibility. Many English teachers do not like to "correct" a Black student's diction. This teacher finds himself or herself in a quandary: a place where no self-respecting educator likes to be. Administrators and parents do not help matters by encouraging social promotion (honoring substandard academic progress in order for the child to pass to the next grade).

It is your duty as a college educated teacher to be courageous. Math, science, and history teachers are correcting their pupils. What makes the English instructor's situation any different? Well, there are unpleasant terms like "correct," "wrong," "right," and "standard" that insult the parents, students, school boards, PTAs, literacy consultants, therapists, and speech pathologists. This is really too bad, because who ends up suffering in the final analysis? The child who is not corrected today will be penalized during future job interviews, at mixed company social gatherings, and for the rest if his or her life. The teacher should not compromise the child's education.

I've seen full-scale arguments develop from this struggle. Parents in some predominantly Black neighborhoods despise teachers who try to correct their child's dialect. I find this ludicrous because the child is in school to learn -- not only about how to speak the language, but to be notified of how to speak and write in cross cultural environments. Can a person maintain his cultural and linguistic identity if he decides to use Standard English in formal situations like school, social events, and in the work place? This becomes a most puzzling question because knowledge of self is an internal volition. Arlette Ingram Willis (University of Illinois at Urbana-Champaign) discusses the concept of the 'self' in an article entitled, *Reading the World of School Literacy: Contextualizing the Experience of a Young African American Male.* She allows us to take a peek into her home, where her school aged son is approached with what she calls unintentional cultural insensitivity. Many teachers adopt and exercise this method and cause in many cases irreparable damage. Willis says, "It [the educational system] is built upon a narrow understanding of school knowledge and literacy, defined and defended as what one needs to know and how one needs to know it in order to be successful in school and society." She eloquently states this scenario as it relates to her child who is Black, trying to cope with one teacher trying to deliberately obliterate race and ethnicity in the classroom: a virtual impossibility. Though the elimination of Black Vernacular English in some mainstream situations may be painful, we find that code switching from one dialect to another is useful not only for (receivers) those who don't understand Black English, but for the senders as well. This echoes the writings of Ellison's *Invisible Man,* DuBois' *The Souls of Black Folks*, and Baldwin's *The Fire Next Time.* Willis goes on to discuss the importance of cultural, functional, and critical forms of literacy. Cultural literacy refers to the network of information all competent readers use, functional being the mastery of skills needed to read and write as measured by standardized forms of assessment, and critical literacy which refers to the ideologies that underlie the relationship between power and knowledge in society. Despite these definitions, the young reader needs to master the reading of letters, words, and paragraphs, before anything else.

Because most Americans learn language during the first 5 years of their lives in a comfortable environment not resembling a school institution, most people have no formal training of the English language. In the stages of being a newborn, an infant, a toddler, and a child, we acquire cues and clues in language. Humans communicate based on needs, and in the earlier stages of life, we acquire our needs by making sounds. As we grow older, societal rules begin to alter the construct of what dialects and sounds are acceptable and efficient for communication. If children are only required to use limited English proficiency, yet receive passing grades in English, this is a form of reward for using sub-standard dialects in class. If a child is never corrected for using fragments, double negatives, slang, misplaced modifiers, and faulty antecedents, what is the purpose of having a language arts curriculum and English teachers? As an educator, teachers are required to give students information within the curriculum and to correct a student's work when it is incorrectly completed. Have American teachers lost their capacity to correct students? If so, we will continue to see a decline in standardized test scores, across the board. Do highly qualified teachers correct students? Do they speak standard English? Do they have high expectations for their students? The answer for all of these should be a resounding, "yes."

EXPERT COMMENTARY ON BLACK ENGLISH

Cruel people take advantage of those who do not know how to read and write.

Dr. Kingsley Fletcher

Studies consistently demonstrate that educators manifest a generally negative reaction to the "less familiar dialect" in favor of Standard English. Black educators have long recognized the possible socioeconomic disadvantages of speaking a Black dialect in a predominantly White society. <u>There is empirically based evidence of teacher bias against Black students.</u> [These children] with this pattern are candidates for coded categories such as "slow learner," "learning disabled," "intellectually impaired" or "not a strong potential candidate." Black English speakers are presented with more obstacles to success than speakers of Standard English.

Betsy Winsboro and Irvin Soloman
Standard English vs. "The American Dream"
Education Digest

Although use of language may not matter in menial jobs, it does matter for the better paying jobs (and for entrance into the professional schools), where employers sometimes are seeking documented reasons for rejecting Blacks.

Darwin Turner
Black Students, Language, and Classroom Teachers
Tapping Potential

Research on the effect of language on employability indicates that, in fact, the better jobs do go to the speakers of Standard English.

> Judy Floyd Robbins
> *Employers' Language Expectations and Nonstandard English*
> English Journal

Yet we must think of Standard English as the common language, the one we use when we want to speak across cultural barriers. And like the workers on the Biblical Tower of Babel, we will be unable to accomplish anything unless we understand one another. Each English has its time and place.

> Daniel Heller
> *The Problem of Standard English*
> English Journal

The neighborhood language becomes what the West Africans call the sweet language. That then makes a person bilingual. He or she speaks Standard English, which is needed in the marketplace. He or she also speaks the sweet language, which is used to make contact with a beloved, a family member, a friend. I think what should be taught is the Standard English language. The other languages of the neighborhood are so in flux that you really can't teach them. You can learn the dialects, but you can't teach them.

> Maya Angelou
> *Slate Newsletter*
> *Support for the Learning and Teaching of English*

Part of the problem could be that individuals look down on people they consider socially inferior.

> Weaver and Eller

The school has seemed unable to recognize and take up the potentially positive interactive and adaptive verbal interpretive habits learned by Black American children, rural and urban, within their families and on the streets. [Black students] have skills that would benefit all youngsters: keen listening and observational skills, quick recognition of roles, rapid-fire dialogue, hard-driving argumentation, succinct recapitulation of an event, striking metaphors, and comparative analyses based on unexpected analogies.

John Baugh, American Psychologist

Remarks and Statistics

Education Week concludes that "most urban 4th graders who live in U.S. cities can't read and understand a simple children's book, and most 8th graders can't use arithmetic to solve a practical problem."

Harvard researcher, Ronald Ferguson found that Blacks watch twice as much television as Whites. (Shaker Heights, Ohio)

"I don't think teachers expect excellence, and you get what you expect."
(An Evanston, Illinois school board member)

Half of American 4th graders spend five hours or more per day watching television...about the same amount of time they spend in classes at school. (NAEP Data Tool)

Only 30% of African Americans take AP courses.

Black teachers, parents, administrators, and students allow underachievement.

Black children study 2 hours less per day than White students.

The Mean Composite S.A.T. Scores
By Major Ethnic Groups in the United States

Race/Ethnicity	Combined
Asian American or Pacific Islander	1070
White (European)	1060
Native American	962
Latin, South, and Central American	922
Puerto Rican	906
Mexican or Mexican American	903
African American	857

The Pennsylvania Report, The College Board
Pennsylvania: Mean SAT Scores, By Race and Ethnicity, 1999

Race/Ethnicity	Verbal	Math	Combined
Asian American or Pacific Islander	484	534	1018
White (European)	509	506	1015
Mexican or Mexican American	482	476	958
Latin, South, and Central American	481	474	955
Native American	461	460	921
Puerto Rican	439	426	865
African American	421	402	823

Education Week

The Gary Indiana Report, Indiana Department of Education
Mean SAT Scores for African Americans in Gary, Indiana, 2003

African Americans	789
Indiana State Average	1004

Garrard McClendon is a writer, professor, professional speaker, and talk show host. He has been an English instructor at the Culver Academies, Bishop Chatard, Bishop Noll Institute, and Purdue University. A graduate of Wabash College and Valparaiso University, McClendon is currently completing his doctoral studies at Loyola University in Chicago. As the GEO Foundation Media Coordinator in northern Indiana, he actively promotes free tutoring initiatives, school improvement, and school choice. McClendon resides with his wife and two children in Northwest Indiana.

www.McClendonReport.com

Teaching one child at a time…